Good Question!

How Many Planets Circle the Sun?

AND OTHER QUESTIONS ABOUT . . .

Our Solar System

STERLING CHILDREN'S BOOKS

New York

STERLING CHILDREN'S BOOKS
New York

An Imprint of Sterling Publishing
387 Park Avenue South
New York, NY 10016

Text © 2014 Mary Kay Carson
Illustrations © 2014 by Sterling Publishing Co., Inc.

Photo Credits: NASA: 9, 10, 12, 15, 17, 21, 22, 25; iStockphoto.com © brainmaster: 1, 2, 3, 7, 10, 12, 17, 21, 25, 30, 31, 32;
© billnoll 4, 5, 9, 13, 15, 18, 22, 24, 26, 27, 29

ISBN 978-1-4549-0668-1 (hardcover)
ISBN 978-1-4549-0669-8 (paperback)

Library of Congress Cataloging-in-Publication Data

Carson, Mary Kay, author.
  How many planets circle the sun? : and other questions about our solar system / Mary Kay Carson.
    pages cm. -- (Good question)
  Audience: K-3.
  Includes bibliographical references and index.
  ISBN 978-1-4549-0669-8 (pbk.) -- ISBN 978-1-4549-0668-1 (hardcover) 1. Solar system--Miscellanea--Juvenile literature.
  2. Planets--Miscellanea--Juvenile literature. I. Title. II. Series: Good question!
  QB501.3.C27 2014
  523.2--dc23

                                                                    2013019124

Distributed in Canada by Sterling Publishing
c/o Canadian Manda Group, 165 Dufferin Street
Toronto, Ontario, Canada M6K 3H6
Distributed in the United Kingdom by GMC Distribution Services
Castle Place, 166 High Street, Lewes, East Sussex, England BN7 1XU
Distributed in Australia by Capricorn Link (Australia) Pty. Ltd.
P.O. Box 704, Windsor, NSW 2756, Australia

Design by Jennifer Browning and Elizabeth Phillips
Illustrations by Ron Miller

For information about custom editions, special sales, and premium and corporate purchases,
please contact Sterling Special Sales at 800-805-5489 or specialsales@sterlingpublishing.com.

Manufactured in China
Lot #:
2 4 6 8 10 9 7 5 3 1
10/13

www.sterlingpublishing.com/kids

CONTENTS

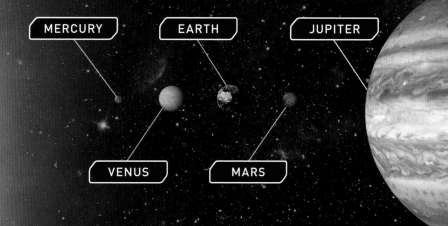

MERCURY

EARTH

JUPITER

VENUS

MARS

How many planets circle the sun?

Eight amazing and unique planets circle our sun—Mercury, Venus, Earth, Mars, Jupiter, Saturn, Uranus, and Neptune. Each planet travels in a path around the sun called an orbit. Mercury, Venus, Earth, and Mars are the inner planets, and they orbit closest to the sun. They are solid and rocky. The outer planets are Jupiter, Saturn, Uranus, and Neptune. They orbit far from the sun's warmth and light. The outer planets are not solid and have no land. Instead, they are made of swirling gases and mushy liquids with small cores of rock or ice.

How can you remember the order of the planets? Here's a helpful phrase: My Very Excellent Mother Just Served Us Nachos. The first letter of each word in the phrase

SATURN

URANUS

NEPTUNE

matches the first letter of each planet in order from the sun—Mercury, Venus, Earth, Mars, Jupiter, Saturn, Uranus, and Neptune.

The eight planets aren't alone in their journey around the sun. Between the solid inner planets and the gassy outer planets is a ring of space rocks. It's called the Asteroid Belt. Comets and dwarf planets also orbit the sun. Bits of ice and rock, planet rings, dust, gas, and more than a hundred moons are all along for the ride, too. All of it together creates a system—a solar system.

What holds our solar system together?

The sun is a ball of hot, glowing gases—a star. It spins and shines in the center of our solar system. The sun produces heat and light. Without it, life on Earth would not be possible. Stars are huge. A million Earths could easily fit inside the sun. Not only is the sun massive, it has 333,000 times the mass of Earth. Mass is the amount of matter, or stuff, something is made of. The sun's huge mass creates a strong pulling force called gravity. The sun's gravity is what keeps the planets circling the sun. The sun pulls the planets, comets, and asteroids into orbit around itself. The massive sun with its powerful gravity is the glue that holds our solar system together. And it's been doing it for 4.5 billion years!

The sun rules our solar system because the sun pretty much *is* our solar system. Our sun contains 99 percent of all the mass in our solar system. The planets, moons, asteroids, comets, gas, dust, and everything else make up less than 1 percent of the solar system. That is extraordinary! But the sun is also quite ordinary. There are billions of stars with the same size and hotness as the sun. But no star is more important to our solar system.

BECAUSE THERE IS NO AIR, THE SKY ABOVE MERCURY'S ROCKY SURFACE IS BLACK, EVEN DURING THE DAY.

Which planet has the shortest year?

If you lived on Mercury, you'd have a birthday every three months. Why? That's how long a year lasts on Mercury. A year is the time it takes a planet to make one orbit around the sun. That trip takes Mercury only 12½ weeks. Mercury is the closest planet to the sun, so its orbit is the shortest. Mercury is both the smallest planet and the fastest—speeding along its orbit at 106,000 miles, or 170,500 kilometers (km), per hour!

While a year zips by on Mercury, a day there drags on and on. A day is the time it takes a planet to complete one spin. Planets spin around, or rotate, like a basketball on a finger. A planet rotates around an imaginary line through its center called an axis. Earth completes one full spin every 24 hours—each Earth day is 24 hours. Mercury rotates slowly, spinning around once every 1,407 hours. That's nearly 60 Earth days!

You could wait a long time to see the sunrise on Mercury, but it would be quite a sight. The sun looks nearly three times larger on Mercury than it does on Earth. Mercury gets ten times more sunlight than Earth during the day. But at night, the temperature can be 1,000 degrees Fahrenheit (1,000°F), or 530 degrees Celsius (530°C), cooler than it is in the daytime. Mercury's rocky cliffs, valleys, and many craters bake during the day and freeze at night. Sunlight never reaches the deepest, darkest craters on Mercury. They stay so cold that ice survives there.

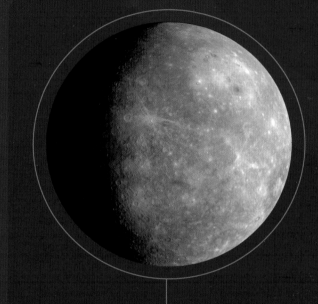

MERCURY IS COVERED IN ANCIENT CRATERS, JUST LIKE OUR MOON.

Which planet in our solar system is the hottest?

Surprisingly, it's not the planet nearest the sun. Mercury is closer to the sun than Venus, but Venus is hotter than Mercury. Why? Venus's heavy air is to blame. The layer of gas surrounding a planet is called an atmosphere. Venus's thick atmosphere of toxic gases is like a heat-trapping blanket. Yellow storm clouds made of acid completely cover the planet. The air on Venus is mostly carbon dioxide. That's the same polluting gas that comes out of car tailpipes and factory smokestacks. Carbon dioxide keeps the second planet blazing hot day and night. How hot? Temperatures reach nearly 900°F (482°C). That's toasty enough to melt some metals! Venus's oceans boiled away long ago.

Venus's atmosphere makes it a difficult place to visit. A few robot spacecraft have landed there, but they didn't last long. The weight of Venus's thick, heavy air crushed them within hours. Odd as it seems, Venus is like Earth in some ways. The two are nearly twins in size and mass. Both planets have mountains and valleys and are made of similar materials. Like Venus's atmosphere, Earth's air has toxic carbon dioxide. Scientists think that pollution is warming our own planet, too.

WALKING ON VENUS WOULD FEEL LIKE BEING 3,000 FEET (914 METERS) UNDERWATER BECAUSE THE AIR IS SO THICK AND HEAVY.

Why is there life on Earth?

So far, life has been found only on Earth. What makes our home planet special? Water and temperatures that keep much of it liquid. Earth's distance from the sun makes its temperature just right for liquid water. Water on Venus turns to steam. Mars is so cold that water stays frozen. Earth orbits between those two planets. Watery oceans, lakes, and rivers cover nearly three-quarters of our planet. All life that we know of—plants, animals, and microbes— depends on water to live and grow.

Earth's distance from the sun provides it with just the right amount of warmth and light. But not all parts of Earth warm equally—or at the same time. Some places are colder during the winter and warmer in the summer. What creates the seasons? Earth's axis is not straight up and down, so our planet spins on a tilt. If Earth were a lollipop on a stick, the stick would lean over a bit. This means that during part of our planet's journey around the sun, the top half of Earth leans toward the sun, creating summer. Meanwhile, the bottom half of Earth is tilted away from the sun and has winter. Half a year later, the opposite happens and the seasons are swapped.

WHAT CAUSES THE SEASONS ON EARTH?

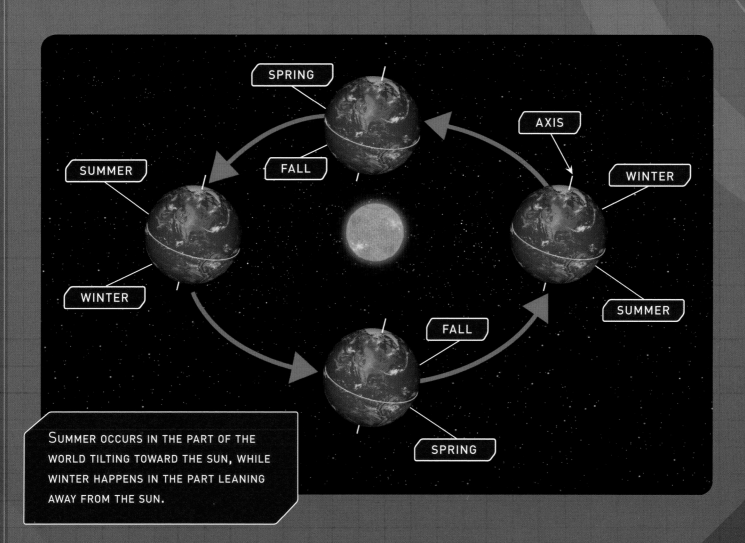

SPRING

FALL

AXIS

SUMMER

WINTER

WINTER

SUMMER

FALL

SPRING

SUMMER OCCURS IN THE PART OF THE WORLD TILTING TOWARD THE SUN, WHILE WINTER HAPPENS IN THE PART LEANING AWAY FROM THE SUN.

Why are there footprints on the moon?

Twelve astronauts walked on the moon between 1969 and 1972. Their footprints are still there. How is that possible? Think about what erases your footprints. Water might wash them away, or blowing dirt could cover them up. On the moon there is no rain, air, or wind. Nothing moves the moon dust, so the footprints remain. An unchanging landscape keeps the moon's ancient craters looking new, too. Craters are big bowl-shaped holes made by space rocks crashing into the surface. The moon is covered in craters that are millions of years old. There's no weather or shifting surface to erase them.

Some of the footprints on the moon are pretty far apart. Astronauts can bounce far and jump high on the moon. Why is moonwalking so much fun? The moon is small and has less gravity than Earth. Normal muscles have superhero strength on the moon! Weaker gravity also means that you weigh less on the moon. A 50-pound (23-kilogram) Earth kid is only an 8½-pound (4-kilogram) moon kid.

A moon is a space object that orbits something larger, such as a planet. There are nearly 150 moons in our solar system. Our moon is the fifth largest. It's a big moon for a planet of Earth's size. Being massive gives the moon's gravity lots of pulling power. As it orbits Earth, the moon's gravity tugs on Earth's oceans. The pull of the moon's gravity creates tides on our planet.

In 1969 Neil Armstrong and Buzz Aldrin became the first astronauts to walk on the moon. This footprint was left by Buzz Aldrin.

OLYMPUS MONS AND OTHER
VOLCANOES ERUPTED ON
MARS LONG AGO.

Are there volcanoes on Mars?

On Mars there's a volcano the size of New Mexico and three times taller than Mount Everest! It's called Olympus Mons. There are dozens of volcanoes on Mars. All are ancient and haven't erupted for many millions of years. Another must-see sight on Mars is a gigantic canyon called Valles Marineris. It's nearly as long as the width of the United States! Mars is covered in interesting stony mountains, sandy craters, and pebbly plains. Although there's a lot to see on Mars, the weather isn't great. Sunny days on the fourth planet don't get above freezing. The air isn't breathable either, and the atmosphere is thin. Today, Mars is a cold, dry desert—but was it always? There are dry riverbeds, ancient lakebeds, and old sea floors all over Mars. Millions of years ago Mars probably was a warmer and wetter world.

How do we know so much about a place 140 million miles away? Robotic spacecraft have been visiting Mars since the 1960s. More than a dozen missions have flown by, orbited around, landed on, or roved over Mars. Spacecraft have taken pictures, tracked weather, tested soil, and studied rocks. There are better maps of Mars's surface than there are of Earth's ocean floor. What secrets is Mars keeping? Current missions are looking for fossils or other signs of past life. Perhaps Mars supported life when it was wetter and warmer.

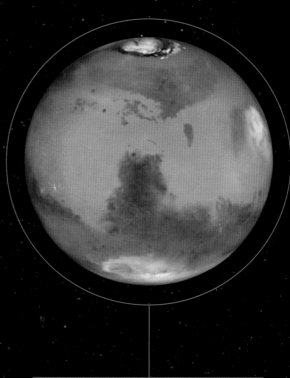

ICE CAPS COVER BOTH THE NORTH AND SOUTH POLES OF MARS.

How wide is the Asteroid Belt?

Asteroids are space rocks—ancient hunks of stone and metal. They were created when our solar system formed nearly 4.5 billion years ago. A ring of asteroids separates the inner and outer planets. It's called the Asteroid Belt and is more than 100 million miles (160 million km) wide. This ring of space rubble orbits around the sun between Mars and Jupiter. Many millions of asteroids travel in the Asteroid Belt. They come in all sorts of odd shapes and look like beat-up potatoes. Some asteroids are hundreds of miles wide and have their own moons. Others are as small as a few city blocks.

Asteroids sometimes get bumped around and broken up into smaller pieces. Small space rocks are called meteoroids. If a meteoroid gets knocked into Earth's atmosphere, it turns into a meteor. Meteors are also called shooting stars or falling stars. Meteors become a streak of burning light as they fall through the atmosphere. Most meteors totally burn up in the air. If what's left of one makes it to the ground, it becomes a meteorite. Rock hunters collect meteorites. Finding one of these heavy metallic rocks is a rare thrill.

An asteroid falling through the atmosphere is not a good thing. Even a small asteroid hitting Earth makes a big mess. An asteroid that slammed into Earth 65 million years ago blasted so much dust into the air that the sky was dark for years. So much sunlight was blocked that Earth's temperature dropped. That colder weather probably killed off the dinosaurs.

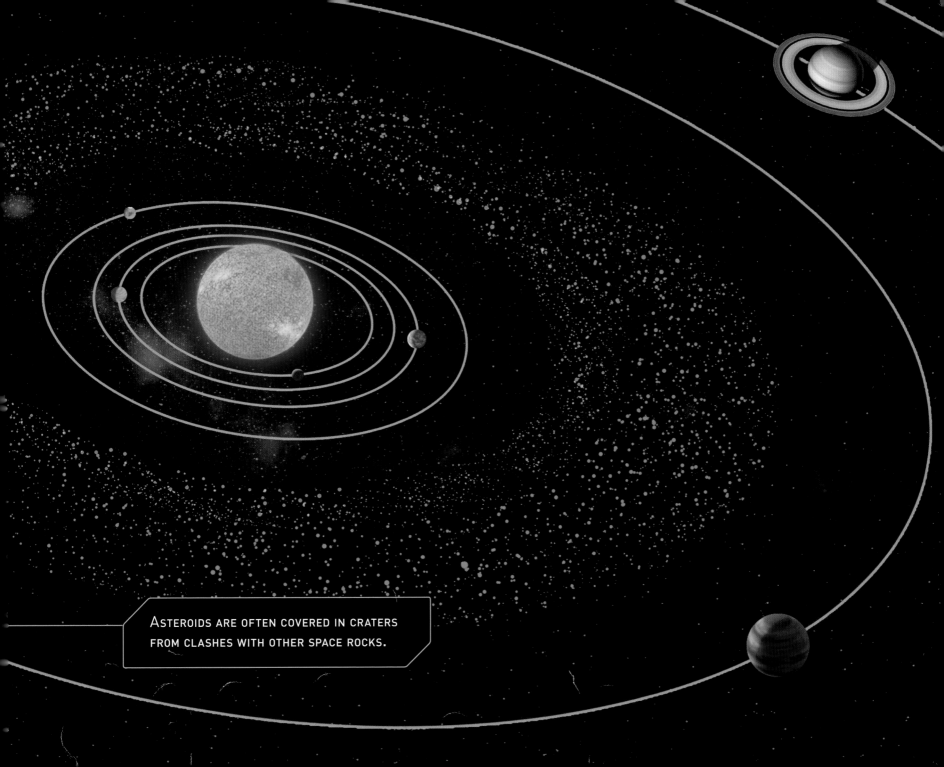

ASTEROIDS ARE OFTEN COVERED IN CRATERS FROM CLASHES WITH OTHER SPACE ROCKS.

Which planet in our solar system is the biggest?

Jupiter is the largest planet and the biggest gas giant. Gas giants are landless planets. They are made up of sloshy liquids and gases and have no solid surface. All of the outer planets—Jupiter, Saturn, Uranus, and Neptune—are gas giants. Jupiter is the most colorful. Stripes and swirls of burnt orange, creamy white, and grayish blue wrap around the giant planet. The bands of color are clouds made of poisonous gases and frozen water. Jupiter has huge storms that look like spinning circles. The Great Red Spot is a storm that's been raging for centuries.

Jupiter is our solar system's most massive planet by far. Jupiter's mass is more than the mass of all the other seven planets put together—and doubled. Jupiter's powerful gravity holds at least 66 moons in orbit. The four biggest of Jupiter's moons—Ganymede, Io, Europa, and Callisto—are like miniature rocky planets. Each is a one-of-a-kind world. Ganymede is bigger than Mercury and is the largest moon in our solar system! Io looks like a splotchy cheese pizza because of all its erupting volcanoes. Europa is about the size of our moon but is covered by a frozen ocean. Callisto is a dead world with an ancient crater-covered surface.

THE GREAT RED SPOT IS A FIERCE STORM MORE THAN TWICE THE SIZE OF EARTH.

How did Saturn get its rings?

Saturn's rings are spectacular. They circle the planet like bright golden hoops. This is why the sixth planet is called the Jewel of the Solar System. All the gas giants have rings—but Jupiter, Uranus, and Neptune have only a few faint, skinny rings. Saturn's rings are wide but thin. Saturn's rings are nearly as wide as the distance between Earth and the moon, but they don't get thicker than a half mile or so.

Rings around planets are made of bits of ice and rock. All of the small pieces speed around the planet in orbit. From a distance the ring of moving chunks look solid. Planets collect the pieces of rock and ice that make up their rings. A big planet's powerful gravity pulls in and grinds up comets, asteroids, and other space stuff. If enough gathered-up stuff gets squashed together within an orbit, a ring can appear.

Why are Saturn's rings so big and bright? Saturn's rings are made of bits of ground-up rock and ice. Scientists even think the rings include rubble from a torn-up moon. Saturn has more than 60 moons. It's likely that long ago a moon came too close to Saturn. The planet's gravity probably broke it up into millions of pieces that kept orbiting and formed rings.

THE *CASSINI* SPACECRAFT TOOK THIS IMAGE IN 2005. IT SHOWS THE SIZES OF THE PARTICLES IN SATURN'S RINGS BY COLOR. THE PURPLE PARTS HAVE THE LARGEST ROCK AND ICE CHUNKS, WHILE THE GREEN AREAS HAVE THE SMALLEST PARTICLES.

THIS IS WHAT A VIEW OF URANUS MIGHT LOOK LIKE FROM ITS MOON, OBERON. URANUS HAS DOZENS OF MOONS, AND OBERON IS THE FARTHEST AWAY.

Which planet used to be named George?

William Herschel was the first person ever to discover a planet. He found the seventh planet in 1781 with a powerful telescope he'd built. All the other planets known at the time—Mercury, Venus, Mars, Jupiter, and Saturn—can be seen without a telescope. Herschel named it the Georgian Planet after England's King George III. It was later renamed after the Greek god of the sky, Uranus.

Unlike any other planet in our solar system, Uranus rotates on its side. Its axis is sideways, and so Uranus spins like a bead on a necklace. Why? No one knows for sure. Scientists think that perhaps something crashed into Uranus and knocked it over long ago.

Which planet has a cloud named Scooter?

Neptune is a dark and stormy place. The eighth planet is probably the windiest in our solar system. Winds whip around Neptune at speeds four times faster than Earth's most destructive tornados. Space scientists gave one of Neptune's fast-moving storm clouds the name Scooter. Why? The speedy cloud patch showed up while a spacecraft was photographing Neptune. Scientists watched as the bright white clouds scooted past a huge hurricane-like storm the size of Earth.

Neptune is very far from the sun. It takes Neptune 165 years to make one trip around the sun. Winter, spring, summer, and autumn last more than 40 years each! Neptune has orbited only once since it was discovered in 1846. Not much of the sun's light and warmth reaches the farthest planet. The sunlight that shines there is 900 times dimmer than the sunlight that reaches Earth.

THIS PHOTO, TAKEN BY THE SPACECRAFT *VOYAGER 2*, SHOWS THE BRIGHT STORM CLOUD NAMED SCOOTER, WHICH ZIPS AROUND NEPTUNE.

What are dwarf planets?

Dwarf planets are similar to the eight planets. They orbit the sun, and some have moons. Dwarf planets are also big enough to be round—unlike smaller comets and asteroids. Anything massive enough ends up as a round ball shape, or sphere. Why? Giant space objects have a lot of gravity squashing them in toward their centers. If a planet is massive enough, gravity acts like giant hands packing a snowball.

Dwarf planets may be sun-circling spheres, but they are different from the eight planets. Planets either collect or scatter nearby objects, such as asteroids, because they are so massive. But a dwarf planet is smaller and weaker. Dwarf planets aren't alone in their path around the sun. The dwarf planet Ceres travels with millions of asteroids in the Asteroid Belt. The other four dwarf planets are out past Neptune—Pluto, Eris, Makemake, and Haumea. It's likely that more objects will be added to the list of planets someday as new discoveries are made.

Are there glowing snowballs in space?

Comets are big, shining icy hunks of frozen rock, gas, and dust—gigantic glowing space snowballs! All comets orbit the sun, and most are the size of small towns. A comet glows when it passes near the sun. The comet warms up, and some of its ice turns into gases. As the comet keeps moving, the gases and dust stream behind it, creating its tail. The comet shines with reflected sunlight, looking like a fuzzy star with a streaky tail.

When a comet comes close to the sun, rocks in the melting ice fly off into space. These small space rocks, or meteoroids, travel around the sun in the comet's orbit. Sometimes when Earth passes through a comet's orbit, we get a nighttime show. A meteor shower is many streaks of light, or meteors, in the night sky over a few days. Meteoroids hit Earth's atmosphere, becoming meteors, and burn up with a flash as they fall. Comets are some of the oldest things around. They are left over from when our solar system formed about 4.5 billion years ago.

Keppler-22b is an exoplanet. It's the perfect distance away from its sun for liquid water to be possible. With more research, we may be able to find out if it can support life.

Are there other planets beyond our solar system?

This book is about our solar system, not *the* solar system. Why is the difference important? Our solar system isn't the only one in the universe! Over the last 25 years, scientists have discovered hundreds of planets circling other stars. Each exoplanet circles an alien sun in a faraway solar system. Exoplanets is the name for planets that orbit other stars. It's short for "extrasolar planets," or planets outside our solar system.

What are exoplanets like? Some are huge, hot gas giants that orbit oddly close to their sun. Others are cold gas giants, and some are small and rocky. There are alien solar systems with as many as seven or more exoplanets in orbit. Are any of these newly found planets like Earth? No one has found another planet like Earth—yet. Another Earth-like planet probably will be found someday. It turns out that exoplanets aren't unusual. Most of the 100 billion or so stars in our galaxy have at least one planet. That's a lot of solar systems to search. What do you think we might find?

Compare the Planets

PLANET	DISTANCE from the sun (million miles/km)	SIZE (miles/km wide)	DAY (hours)	YEAR (Earth days)	MOONS/ RINGS
Mercury	36/58	3,032/4,879	1,407	88	0/0
Venus	67/108	7,521/12,104	5,832	225	0/0
Earth	93/150	7,918/12,742	24	365	1/0
Mars	142/228	4,212/6,779	24½	687	2/0
Jupiter	484/778	86,881 /139,822	10	4,331	66/4
Saturn	886/1,427	72,367/116,464	10½	10,756	62/7
Uranus	1,784/2,871	31,518/50,724	17¼	30,687	27/13
Neptune	2,795/4,498	30,599/49,244	16	60,190	13/6

Find Out More

WEBSITES TO VISIT

NASA SPACE PLACE
http://spaceplace.nasa.gov/menu/solar-system
Play Mission to Jupiter, Cosmic Colors, and other games; explore pictures and questions about the solar system; and find fun activities and science fair projects to do.

SKY WATCHING
http://stardate.org/nightsky/
http://www.skyandtelescope.com/observing/ataglance
http://amazing-space.stsci.edu/tonights_sky/
You can see a lot of our solar system from here on Earth. These websites will help you find planets, meteor showers, and the phases of the moon in the night sky.

SOLAR SYSTEM EXPLORATION
http://solarsystem.nasa.gov/kids
This kid-friendly destination has Homework Helper pages about the sun, eight planets, comets, and everything else in our solar system written just for students.

BOOKS TO READ

Aguilar, David A. *13 Planets: The Latest View of the Solar System*. National Geographic, 2011.

Carson, Mary Kay. *Far-Out Guide to Asteroids and Comets*. Enslow, 2010.

Loewen, Nancy. *Dwarf Planets: Pluto, Charon, Ceres, and Eris*. Picture Window Books, 2008.

Siy, Alexandra. *Cars on Mars: Roving the Red Planet*. Charlesbridge, 2009.

Trammel, Howard K. *The Solar System*. Children's Press, 2009.

Wittenstein, Vicki Oransky. *Planet Hunter, Geoff Marcy and the Search for Other Earths*. Boyds Mills Press, 2010.

For bibliography and free activities visit:
http://www.sterlingpublishing.com/kids/good-question

INDEX